QUALITY CUSTOMER SERVICE FOR FRONT LINE STAFF

Better Management Skills

This highly popular range of inexpensive paperbacks covers all areas of basic management. Practical, easy to read and instantly accessible, these guides will help managers to improve their business or communication skills. Those marked * are available on audio cassette.

The books in this series can be tailored to specific company requirements. For further details, please contact the publisher, Kogan Page, telephone 0171 278 0433, fax 0171 837 6348.

Be a Successful Supervisor
Business Etiquette
Coaching Your Employees
Conducting Effective Interviews
Counselling Your Staff
Creative Decision-making
Creative Thinking in Business
Delegating for Results
Effective Employee Participation
Effective Meeting Skills
Effective Performance Appraisals*
Effective Presentation Skills
Empowerment
First Time Supervisor
Get Organised!
Goals and Goal Setting
How to Communicate Effectively*
How to Develop a Positive
  Attitude*
How to Develop Assertiveness
How to Motivate People*
How to Understand Financial
  Statements
How to Write a Staff Manual
Improving Employee
  Performance
Improving Relations at Work
Keeping Customers for Life
Leadership Skills for Women
Learning to Lead

Make Every Minute Count*
Making TQM Work
Managing Cultural Diversity at
  Work
Managing Disagreement
  Constructively
Managing Organisational Change
Managing Part-Time Employees
Managing Your Boss
Marketing for Success
Memory Skills in Business
Mentoring
Office Management
Personnel Testing
Productive Planning
Project Management
Quality Customer Service
Rate Your Skills as a Manager
Sales Training Basics
Self-managing Teams
Selling Professionally
Successful Negotiation
Successful Presentation Skills
Successful Telephone Techniques
Systematic Problem-solving and
  Decision-making
Team Building
Training Methods that Work
The Woman Manager

QUALITY CUSTOMER SERVICE FOR FRONT LINE STAFF

William B Martin

KOGAN PAGE

First published in the United States of America in 1986; revised 1988
by Crisp Publications Inc, 1200 Hamilton Court, Menlo Park, California
94025, USA.

This edition first published in Great Britain in 1988 by Kogan Page Ltd,
120 Pentonville Road, London N1 9JN

Reprinted 1995, 1996

British Library Cataloguing in Publication Data

A CIP record for this book is available from the British Library.

ISBN 0–7494–1247–X

Typeset by BookEns Ltd. Baldock, Herts.
Printed and bound in Great Britain by Clays Ltd, St Ives plc.

Contents

About This Book

This book is for people who currently work, or plan to work, in a job that requires interaction with customers from outside the organisation as well as inside. It is addressed to the front-line employee who ultimately determines the quality level of customer service. The material was designed to make sure that all points of customer contact – those 'moments of truth' – occur in the best way possible. In short, this book may be used by an organisation that wants to teach employees how to provide quality customer service.

The premiss of this book is twofold: quality customer service is the key to success for any employee with customer service responsibility, and quality customer service is the foundation upon which an organisation's success and profits are built.

Unfortunately, a majority of organisations concentrate on the technical side of job performance and devote far too little time to the 'people side' of business. Training is often catch-as-catch-can because of limited resources, busy schedules and a lack of time. Also, many service supervisors are not experienced enough to train employees properly in effective customer-relation skills.

This programme is useful for training new employees as well as promoting the continued development of more experienced personnel. All that is required is an interested employee, a pencil and some time. Using *Quality Customer Service* and follow-up on the part of the manager or trainer will provide measurably improved customer service for any organisation.

Is This Book for You?

This book is for *you* if your job requires you to interact with other people. The people with whom you may interact fall into two groups: internal and external.

If you provide service to either one or both of these groups, they are your customers.

> Internal customers are people inside your organisation who depend on you for service.
>
> External customers are people outside your organisation who depend on you for service.

Common names used to describe internal customers:

- the accounts department
- my boss
- colleagues
- engineering
- the people in operations
- data processing
- the marketing department
- production
- the lab
- the people on the third floor.

Common names used to describe external customers:

- customers
- clients
- patients
- guests
- students
- constituents
- stakeholders
- passengers.

Who are your customers? What do you call them?
Name some of your *internal* customers here. (They may be individuals, groups, departments and/or allied organisations.)

_____

_____

Name some of your *external* customers here. (They may be individuals, groups or entire organisations.)

_____

_____

To the Reader

The person who gave you this book wants you to read it carefully, working through all the exercises and activities. If you have any problems as you proceed, ask your trainer/supervisor for assistance.

Once you have read the book, and completed its exercises, you will be better prepared to practise the secrets of quality customer service. What you learn, and the subsequent changes this programme brings, are far more important than the time it takes to finish. Read slowly and think about each point as it is introduced because it is there for you.

Interacting with customers should be fun and challenging. Ideally, you should enjoy interacting with the people with whom your job brings you in contact.

Dealing effectively with people requires many principles, methods and skills which need to be recognised, learned and practised. Therefore, the way to make the most of your job is to enjoy it as fully as possible and learn all you can about the process. It is the combination of your attitude and your skills that will determine the kind of customer service you provide for your employer. *Quality Customer Service* can help to make you a winner!

Good luck!

William B Martin

CHAPTER 1

Do You Have What it Takes to Provide Outstanding Quality Customer Service?

The people in your organisation think so, or they wouldn't have taken you on. Now is the time to prove them correct.

Miss Johnson:
Please explain
to these nice people
how they all ended up
in suite 124.

Make your choice now

Service successes	Service failures
Those with a positive attitude and cheerful outlook	Those who seem depressed or angry
Those who genuinely enjoy working with and for other people	Those who would rather work alone or with 'things'
Those with the ability to put the customer on 'centre stage' rather than themselves	Those who need to be the centre of attention
Those with a high energy level and who enjoy a fast pace	Those who work at their own relaxed pace
Those who view their job primarily as a human relations profession	Those who consider technical aspects of the job more important than customer satisfaction
Those who are flexible and enjoy new demands and experiences	Those who must have things happen in an orderly and predictable way
Those who can allow customers to be right (even on those occasions when they are not)	Those who need others to know that they are right
Add your own:	Add your own:
———————————	———————————
———————————	———————————
———————————	———————————
———————————	———————————
———————————	———————————

> Differences between effective and ineffective service are a matter of sensitivity, sincerity, attitude and human relations skills – all of which can be learned.

It isn't enough simply to perform the duties of your job. You must also have the right approach.

- A patient in a doctor's waiting room wants more than treatment.
- Airline passengers want more than a safe flight.
- Clients in a transaction want more than a settlement.
- Customers in a large store want more than a product.
- Guests in hotels want more than a room.
- Restaurant patrons want more than a meal.
- Car rental customers want more than a car.

Customers want more than just the product or service that is offered. They also want to be treated well!

How good are your service skills? Remember, quality customer service providers are made, not born.

Customer relations: potential scale

I control my moods most of the time	10 9 8 7 6 5 4 3 2 1	I have limited control over my moods.
It is possible for me to be pleasant to people who are indifferent to me.	10 9 8 7 6 5 4 3 2 1	I simply can't be pleasant if people are not nice to me.
I like most people and enjoy meeting others.	10 9 8 7 6 5 4 3 2 1	I have difficulty getting along with others.
I enjoy being of service to others.	10 9 8 7 6 5 4 3 2 1	People should help themselves.
I do not mind apologising for mistakes even if I did not make them.	10 9 8 7 6 5 4 3 2 1	Apologising for a mistake I didn't make is wrong.
I take pride in my ability to communicate verbally with others.	10 9 8 7 6 5 4 3 2 1	I would rather interact with others in writing.
I'm good at remembering names and faces, and make efforts to improve this skill when meeting others.	10 9 8 7 6 5 4 3 2 1	Why bother remembering a name or face if you will never see that person again?
Smiling comes naturally to me.	10 9 8 7 6 5 4 3 2 1	I am more serious by nature.
I like seeing others enjoy themselves.	10 9 8 7 6 5 4 3 2 1	I have no motivation to please others, especially those I don't know.
I keep myself clean and well groomed.	10 9 8 7 6 5 4 3 2 1	Being clean and well groomed is not all that important.

TOTAL SCORE _____

If you rated yourself 80 or above, you are probably excellent with customers, clients or guests. If you rated yourself between 50 and 80, you may need to learn better human relations skills before working with the public. If you scored under 50, working with customers is probably a poor career choice for you.

What is quality customer service?
Two primary dimensions make up quality customer service: the *procedural* dimension and the *personal* dimension. Each is critical to the delivery of quality service.

- *The procedural side* of service consists of the established systems and procedures to deliver products and/or service.
- *The personal side* of service is how service personnel, (using their attitudes, behaviour and verbal skills) interact with customers.

The exercises and activities in this book reflect both dimensions of quality service.

Quality service exercise

The diagrams below show the procedural and personal dimensions of service in graphic form.

The vertical axis represents the degree of procedural service and the horizontal axis reflects a measure of personal service.

Study each diagram. How would you describe the nature of the service reflected in each diagram? Indicate your responses in the spaces provided.

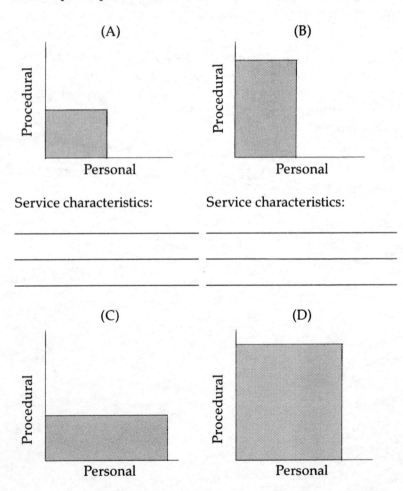

(A)

Procedural

Personal

Service characteristics:

_____

_____

_____

(B)

Procedural

Personal

Service characteristics:

_____

_____

_____

(C)

Procedural

Personal

(D)

Procedural

Personal

Service characteristics: Service characteristics:

_____   _____

_____   _____

_____   _____

The author's response to each diagram follows:

Four types of service

Diagram A   This reflects an operation that is low in both per-
The Freezer   sonal and procedural service. This 'freezer'
approach to service communicates to customers,
'We don't care.'

(A)

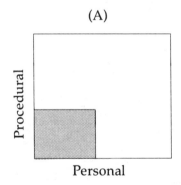

Personal

The 'freezer' service characteristics:

Procedural	**Personal**
slow	insensitive
inconsistent	cold or impersonal
disorganised	apathetic
chaotic	aloof
inconvenient	uninterested

Message to customers: 'We don't care.'

Diagram B
The Factory
This diagram represents proficient procedural service but a weakness in the personal dimension. This 'factory' approach to service communicates to customers, 'You are a number. We are here to process you.'

(B)

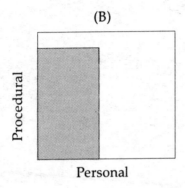

Procedural

Personal

The 'factory' service characteristics:

Procedural	**Personal**
prompt	insensitive
efficient	apathetic
uniform	aloof
	uninterested

Message to customers: 'You are a number. We are here to process you.'

Diagram C
The Friendly Zoo

The 'friendly zoo' approach to service is very personal but lacks procedural consistency. This type of service communicates to customers, 'We are trying hard, but don't really know what we're doing.'

(C)

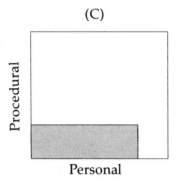

Personal

The 'friendly zoo' service characteristics:

Procedural	Personal
slow	friendly
inconsistent	pleasing
disorganised	interested
chaotic	tactful

Message to customers: 'We are trying hard, but we don't really know what we're doing.'

Diagram D This diagram represents *quality customer service*. It
QCS   is strong in both the personal and procedural
           dimensions. It communicates to customers, 'We
           care and we deliver.'

(D)

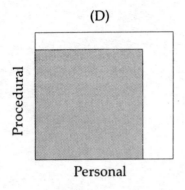

Personal

Quality customer service characteristics:

Procedural   **Personal**
prompt   friendly
efficient   pleasing
uniform   interested
                    tactful

Message to customers: 'We care, and we deliver!'

Four reasons why quality service is important

1. Growth of the service industry
There are more businesses providing services than ever
before. Almost half of UK businesses are service related and
employ approximately one-third of the total workforce. The
growth of service-related organisations continues to expand.

2. Increased competition

Whether it's the corner service station, Joe's Plumbing Service, a giant retail outlet, or an international bank, competition is keen. Business survival depends on obtaining the competitive edge. Quality customer service provides the competitive advantage for thousands of organisations.

3. Greater understanding of consumers

We know more today than ever before about why customers patronise certain services and avoid others. Quality products, along with a realistic price, are a must; but that's not all. Customers also want to be treated well and do repeat business with places that emphasise service.

4. Quality customer service makes economic sense

The lifeblood of any company is repeat business. Expanding the customer base is vital. This means companies not only have to attract new clients or customers, but must also keep existing ones. Quality customer service helps to make this happen.

Following is a list of some organisations that benefit from 'quality customer service'.

Hotels	Travel and tour-related businesses
Banks	Clubs
Restaurants	Supermarkets
Department stores	Service and repair companies
Retail outlets	Utility companies
Hospitals	Local authorities
Insurance companies	Finance and brokerage businesses
Libraries	Solicitors' offices
Doctors' surgeries	Police departments
Universities	Construction companies
Security services	Government agencies

Is your type of organisation represented above?

Should it be?

Why success in customer relations is important to you

Common sense should tell you that the success you have with customers will increase the amount of money you make, whether in salary increases, commission or tips, as well as make you more promotable. Money aside, success in customer relations also provides many *personal* benefits.

Read each statement below. Determine which are *true* and which are *false* about the benefits good customer relations skills can bring to you.

(Check your answers with those of the author on page 27.)

True or False

_____ 1. Working with customers is usually more enjoyable than working at a routine technical job.

_____ 2. Improving interpersonal skills can help to develop a personality.

_____ 3. The ability to provide the best possible customer service is a continuous challenge that keeps a job interesting.

_____ 4. Most top executives lack effective customer-relations skills.

_____ 5. Ongoing success with customers can lead to better job security and opportunity for promotion.

_____ 6. Learning to treat customers as special people has a 'carry over' value to future jobs.

_____ 7. What you learn about customer/client services in an entry level position is often more important than the money you make.

_____ 8. Service jobs where you meet the public are easier than most technical jobs.

_____ 9. Skill in performing the mechanics of your job is more important than your attitude about how you perform it.

_____ 10. Smiles are contagious.

Answers: 1. T 2. T 3. T 4. F (Many top executives use effective guest-relations skills to get them to the top.) 5. T 6. T 7. T 8. F (Guest-relations jobs are more demanding because they require you to stay positive all the time.) 9. F (Your attitude is at least as important as your job skills.) 10. T

Quality customer service

Treating customers professionally is like playing a game of cricket.

1. Like cricket, it is sometimes possible to do everything right and still not win.
2. But your *customer service batting average* will increase when you *cover the wicket the right way;* and
3. When customers, clients and/or guests *return* because they have been treated well, you know you have *scored.*

CHAPTER 2
Four Steps to Quality Customer Service

STEP 1: SEND A POSITIVE ATTITUDE TO OTHERS

Attitude
1. An attitude is a state of mind influenced by feelings, thought and action tendencies.
2. The attitude you send out is usually the attitude you get back.

Alison was a disagreeable sort. Her fellow workers at the supermarket where she was a checker found her moody. Customers did not appreciate her sour disposition, and a few said so to the manager. When business took a temporary downturn, it came as no surprise when Alison was the first to be laid off.

How positive is your attitude?

Most customer service employees who fail do so because of poor *attitude*. Nothing in customer service is better than *sending a positive attitude* to all with whom you come in contact.

The attitude you project to others depends primarily on the

way you look at your job. To measure your attitude towards others, complete this exercise.

Circle the extent you agree or disagree with each statement.

		Agree				Disagree
1.	There is nothing demeaning about assisting or serving others.	5	4	3	2	1
2.	I can be cheerful and positive with everyone regardless of age or appearance.	5	4	3	2	1
3.	On bad days when nothing goes right, I can still find ways to be positive.	5	4	3	2	1
4.	The higher the quality of service I provide during work, the better I feel.	5	4	3	2	1
5.	I am enthusiastic about my job.	5	4	3	2	1
6.	Encountering difficult 'people' situations from time to time will not cause me to be negative	5	4	3	2	1
7.	The idea of being a professional at customer contact is motivating.	5	4	3	2	1
8.	Performing a 'people-oriented' job is both challenging and fun.	5	4	3	2	1
9.	I feel great pleasure when others compliment me or my organisation on superior service.	5	4	3	2	1
10.	Doing well in all aspects of my job is very important to me.	5	4	3	2	1

TOTAL SCORE _____

If you scored above 40, you have an excellent attitude towards your job. If you scored between 25 and 40, you seem to have some reservations that should be examined before you make a career which involves customer contact. A rating below 25 indicates a non-customer relations job would probably be best for you.

Step 1
One good way to send a positive attitude is by **your appearance.**

You never get a *second* chance to create a positive *first* impression. There may be no opportunity for a second impression!

Communicating your best image

Like an actor or actress, interacting with others requires you to be on stage at all times. Creating a good first impression is essential. It is also important to understand that there is a direct connection between how you look to yourself and your attitude. The better your self-image when you encounter customers, clients or guests, the more positive you will be.

Rate yourself on each grooming area presented below. If you circle a 5 you are saying that improvement is not required. If you circle a 1 or 2 you need considerable improvement. Be honest.

	Excellent	Good	Fair	Weak	Poor
Hairstyle, hair grooming (appropriate length and cleanliness)	5	4	3	2	1
Personal habits of cleanliness (body)	5	4	3	2	1
Personal habits of cleanliness (hands, fingernails and teeth)	5	4	3	2	1
Clothing and jewellery (appropriate to the situation)	5	4	3	2	1
Neatness (shoes shined, clothes clean, well pressed, etc)	5	4	3	2	1

	Excellent	Good	Fair	Weak	Poor
General grooming: Will your appearance reflect professionalism on the job?	5	4	3	2	1

When it comes to appearance on the job, I would rate myself:

☐ Excellent   ☐ Good   ☐ Need improvement

> The most successful people in customer contact jobs claim that to be sharp mentally means communicating a positive self-image.

Step 1

Send a positive attitude by your **Body Language**.

Did you know that body language can account for more than half of the message you communicate?

Here is a body language checklist. Tick the square if you can answer 'Yes' to the question.

☐ Do you hold your head high and steady?

☐ Do your arms move in a natural, unaffected manner?

☐ Are your facial muscles relaxed and under control?

☐ Do you find it easy to maintain a natural smile?

☐ Is your body movement controlled, neither harried nor too casual?

☐ Do you find it easy to maintain eye contact with people you are talking to?

Body language exercise

Four sets of opposite non-verbal messages are presented below.

Can you describe the possible messages these forms of body language send to guests?

Positive messages	Negative messages
Face is relaxed and under control.	Face is anxious and uptight.
This communicates _____	This communicates _____
_____	_____
_____	_____
Smile is natural and comfortable.	Smile is missing or forced.
This communicates _____	This communicates _____
_____	_____
_____	_____
Eye contact is maintained when talking and listening to others.	Eye contact is avoided when talking and listening.
This communicates _____	This communicates _____
_____	_____
_____	_____
Body movement is relaxed, yet deliberate and controlled.	Body movement is harried and rushed.
This communicates _____	This communicates _____
_____	_____
_____	_____

Compare your comments with those of the author on page 87.

Step 1

Send a positive attitude by the **sound of your voice.**

The tone of your voice, or *how* you say something, is often more important than the words you use.

> Charlie is a ten-year veteran on the local police force. As a foot patrolman in one of the toughest parts of town, he developed an authoritarian and intimidating tone to his voice. Now that Charlie has been transferred to community affairs, he has had to learn to adjust his voice to project a more conciliatory and friendly image.

Listening to the sound of your own voice

The tone of voice you use with others may mean the difference between:

1. Acceptable job success and *great* job success; and
2. Adequate customer service and *quality* customer service.

Listed below are different voice styles by which people communicate. Which seem to describe yours best? Tick those with which you identify most.

_____ My voice becomes agitated and/or loud when I am angry.

_____ I speak more quickly when nervous.

_____ My voice slows significantly and/or becomes quieter when I get tired.

_____ Others describe my tone of voice as 'lively'.

_____ Friends regard my tone of voice as warm and understanding when we are in a serious conversation.

_____ I can control my tone of voice in most situations.

_____ My voice can sound authoritarian and demanding when required.

_____ Others consider my voice meek.

_____ I'm lucky because my voice is clear, direct and natural.

_____ My vocabulary and style of speaking tends to be serious and scholarly.

Some of the above are better than others when interacting with customers. Please review the comments of the author on page 88.

Note. This may be a difficult exercise for those not accustomed to listening to themselves. Ask a friend to help you complete this exercise; it may provide some invaluable insights. Use of a tape recorder or telephone answering device can also be helpful.

Step 1
Send a positive attitude when **using the telephone**.
   Skill on the telephone is important because:

1. You have only your voice to rely on. Body language, written messages and visual aids are unavailable.
2. When you are on the phone with a customer or client, you are _the_ single representative of your company. In other words, _you are your organisation._

Question: True or false? When you answer the phone with a smile on your face, the tone of your voice will communicate a positive attitude to the person calling you.

Answer: True.

Telephone quiz

Treating customers professionally means being as pleasant over the phone as you are in person. Take the telephone quiz below and see if you can score 100 per cent.

True or False

_____ 1. It is all right to keep someone waiting on the phone while you attend to another equally important task.

_____ 2. You should actually smile when you answer the telephone.

_____ 3. If nobody is around to answer a ringing phone and it is not your assigned job, the best thing to do is let it ring.

_____ 4. It is acceptable not to return a call. If the call was important, the caller will try again.

_____ 5. If a customer is rude, it is your right to be equally snippy.

_____ 6. You should identify yourself by name when answering a business-related telephone call.

_____ 7. If business is slow, it is perfectly acceptable to make personal calls to your friends.

_____ 8. It is important to communicate a sincere interest in the caller and the information that is being requested or provided.

_____ 9. The conversation should be ended in a positive manner, with a summary of any action to be taken.

_____ 10. When you are upset, it is possible to communicate a negative attitude over the phone without realising it.

Step 1

Send a positive attitude by **staying energised.**

Three customer-service *myths:*

1. Customer service is less tiring than other jobs that require hard physical labour.
2. Providing *quality* customer service every day – all the time – is easy.
3. If you can be helpful and friendly to one customer, you will find it just as easy to treat hundreds of customers the same way.

Customer-service *realities:*

1. Customer service requires the exertion of *emotional labour.* Emotional labour takes its toll of your energy level just as physical labour does; that is, it makes you tired.
2. The ideas and concepts presented in this book are simple to understand, but that does not mean that they are necessarily easy to accomplish every day, all the time. Providing quality customer service on a regular basis can be very challenging.
3. Serving many customers over an extended period can be very tiring. When you have exhausted your reservoir of emotional energy, it is called *contact overload syndrome.*

   When you are suffering from contact overload syndrome you can become:

   - Tired
   - Listless
   - Dejected
   - Grouchy/impatient
   - Even clumsy.

Each of these conditions *reduces* your ability to provide *quality customer service.*

Is contact overload syndrome a potential problem for you?

If so, how?

_____

_____

_____

_____

_____

_____

_____

_____

When you are *emotionally tired*, what can you do to *re-energise yourself?*

_____

_____

_____

_____

_____

_____

_____

Still going . . . but for how long?

We all need our batteries recharged from time to time!

Your ability to re-energise yourself is important to maintaining a positive attitude towards your customers.

Maintaining your *positive attitude* is your *key* to delivering *quality customer service* every minute on the job.

Why send a positive attitude?

1. *Customer relations is an integral part of your job – not an extension of it.*
   Nothing is more important to your company than customers. Without them, your company could not exist.

2. *Satisfied customers are essential to the success of your organisation.*
   Business grows through satisfied customers. Satisfied customers not only come back, but they also bring their friends.

3. *Quality customer care is learned not inherited.*
   Like mastering any skill, being able to excel in customer care requires practice and experience. The more you put into it, the more you will receive from it.

'In other companies where I have worked, the maintenance departments made me feel guilty about calling them for help. But here, the people in maintenance are a joy to work with. No matter what time of day or night, no matter what the problem is, they are always smiling and willing to help. That makes my job a lot easier.'

Office worker

Case 1
Customer contact

Thelma's performance appraisal

Thelma works in a fast-food restaurant on the counter. Here is what Thelma's manager had to say on her last performance appraisal:

'Thelma is extremely conscientious about getting her work done. She follows the outlined procedures exactly. She can be relied on to get a job done quickly and efficiently. She often works overtime and does so without complaining. She is a hard worker who strives to do the technical part of her job right, and is highly productive.

'However, when it comes to interacting with customers, Thelma needs considerable improvement. She often fails to see their point of view or consider their feelings. She sometimes acts as though customers are an irritation interrupting her work. She is regarded by some as uncaring and tends to be inflexible when they request extra service.

'If her performance continues, it will be necessary to reposition Thelma to the laundry where customer contact is limited.'

Questions	Answers
1. Is Thelma a good employee? Explain.	_____ _____ _____
2. Is the manager justified in his recommendations? Why or why not?	_____ _____ _____

3. What suggestions would you
   make to Thelma? _____
   _____
   _____

(See the author's comments on page 88)

Step 1 Summary and follow-up

Summary
Reflecting a positive attitude in your job is nothing more than *really* liking your job and allowing your *actions* and *words* to broadcast this enjoyment to your customers, supervisors and fellow employees.

Positive attitudes are shown in your:

☐ Appearance
☐ Body language
☐ The sound of your voice; and
☐ Telephone skills.

Make sure all these reflect a positive attitude from you and check each one that still needs work on your part. Practice makes perfect.

Follow-up
You have now completed Step 1 of this programme. This is a good time to sit down with your manager and/or trainer and talk about what you have learned. This is also a good time to clarify any questions you may have about the job.

Make notes about what you want to discuss and/or your questions.

Things to discuss

1. Questions to my manager about our customers.
2. Questions to colleagues about procedures and routines.
3. Some of 'my ideas'.
4. Follow-up based on discussion.
5. Other.

STEP 2: IDENTIFY THE NEEDS OF YOUR CUSTOMERS, GUESTS OR CLIENTS

Chain of command: the customer is the boss.

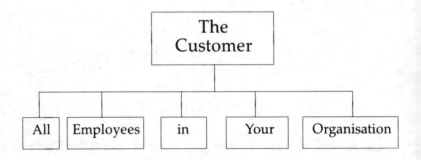

It is important for you to know:

- What your customers want
- What your customers need
- What your customers think
- What your customers feel

- Whether your customers are satisfied
- Whether your customers will return.

How well can you identify these basic human needs?

Human needs

Following is a list of common human needs. Tick those that reflect the needs of *your* customers, guests or clients.

☐   1. The need to feel welcome.

☐   2. The need for prompt service.

☐   3. The need to feel comfortable.

☐   4. The need for orderly service.

☐   5. The need to be understood.

☐   6. The need to receive help or assistance.

☐   7. The need to feel important.

☐   8. The need to be appreciated.

☐   9. The need to be recognised or remembered.

☐ 10. The need for respect.

Give yourself a perfect score if you ticked all 10 items. All customers, regardless of your business or operation, have these basic human needs to some degree.

Step 2
Identify customer, guest or client needs by knowing the **timing requirements** for quality customer service.

Harry is sales manager at a large car dealership. Since the dealer makes money from the service department, Harry plays a crucial role in the overall success of the company. One thing that Harry has done to build new business and convert it to repeat business is a new system to expedite the taking of service orders first thing in the morning. Since most customers drop their car off on the way to work, getting customers processed as quickly as possible is important. Meeting his customers' timing needs is just one way Harry has built his service department into the busiest one in the area.

Timeliness

How timely should you be?
Knowing the service time requirements for your operation is critical to performing quality service.

Five important personal contact points are listed below. There is also space for your manager/trainer to add additional items specific to your situation.

Indicate what you think the response time should be for each item. Then ask your supervisor or trainer to do the same.

Once you have completed the exercise, try to discuss the timing needs of your job with your trainer or supervisor.

	Your response	**Supervisor's response**

Personal contact point:

1. A customer approaches the service area. He/She should be greeted, or have his/her presence acknowledged within _____ seconds. _____ _____

	Your response	Supervisor's response

Personal contact point:

2. The initial paperwork or transaction should be completed within _____ minutes.

3. Any follow-up paperwork or transaction should be completed within _____ minutes.

4. Special requests should be handled within _____ or the guest, customer or client notified of the reason for the delay.

5. Telephone calls should be answered within _____ rings.

6. Other; specify _____

See author's comments on page 88.

> A major university was experiencing declining student enrolments. Upon investigating the problem, they discovered that they were taking much longer than other universities to respond to applications for admission. Prospective students were choosing to attend universities that responded to their applications more promptly.

Step 2
Anticipate customer needs by being **one step ahead** of your clients, customers, guests or patients.

Bob and Ruth are nurses. They work for different doctors at the same clinic. Before each day begins, Ruth goes over the appointment list and makes sure that potentially needed supplies, equipment and medication are at her immediate disposal. Bob, on the other hand, attends to his patients' needs as they are treated. It is not surprising that Ruth finishes her patient load long before Bob.

Anticipate the needs of your customers, guests, or clients.

Ask yourself:
'Have I considered all of the customer's needs?'
'What will the guest need next?'
'How can I improve service now for my client?'

Then offer or provide that service, *without requiring a customer to ask for it!*

Five common service situations are listed below. After each, write in the space provided what you think is needed next.

After you complete the five specified situations, add five of your own, or ask your supervisor/trainer to add to the list.

Situation   **Anticipated need**

1. A customer has waited longer
   than normal for service.   _____

   _____

2. The client keeps glancing at
   his watch.   _____

   _____

3. A woman guest with three
   small children approaches
   your service area. _____

   _____

4. Queues for your service form
   early in the day. _____

   _____

5. There are well-defined busy
   periods in your working day. _____

   _____

Others' needs specific to your situation:

6. _____   _____

7. _____   _____

8. _____   _____

9. _____   _____

10. _____   _____

(See author's comments on page 89.)

'Proper anticipation is the key to my day-to-day success.
Without it, I'm out of business in no time.'

A restaurant manager

Step 2

Identify customer needs through your **attentiveness.**

Attentiveness is the skill of understanding what your customers
may need and want. It goes beyond promptness and anticipation
because it requires you to tune-in to the human needs of your
customers.

Reading your customer

1. Reading the customer requires sensitivity
Reading the customer requires being sensitive to both non-verbal and verbal signals that customers send out (sometimes without being aware).

Here are some common signals. Can you think of customer needs the following signals might be communicating?

Signal		Possible customer need
Age of customer:	Young	_____
	Old	_____
Type of clothing:	High fashion	_____
	Out of fashion	_____
	Worn out	_____
Verbal ability:	Extremely fluent	_____
	Barely fluent	_____
Attitude:	Positive	_____
	Negative	_____
Impatient		_____
Demanding or angry		_____

Compare your customers with those of the author on page 89.

2. Reading the customer requires empathy
Empathy is what *understanding* is all about. This means putting yourself in the position of your customers. You must view the situation through 'their eyes'. You must ask, 'If I were this person, what would I want?'

Do you have the ability to be empathetic to your customers, clients or guests?

_____ Yes _____ No

Why do you think so? _____

_____

Step 2
Identify needs by **understanding basic customer needs**.

Just like you, customers need: help, respect, comfort, empathy, satisfaction, support, and a friendly face.

Four basic needs

1. The need to be understood
Those who select your service need to feel they are communicating effectively. This means the messages they send should be interpreted correctly. Emotions or language barriers can get in the way of proper understanding.

2. The need to feel welcome
Anyone doing business with you who feels like an outsider will not return. People need to feel you are happy to see them and that their business is important to you.

3. The need to feel important
Ego and self-esteem are powerful human needs. We all like to feel important. Anything you can do to make a guest feel special is a step in the right direction.

4. The need for comfort
Customers need physical comfort, a place to wait, rest, talk or do business. They also need psychological comfort, the assurance they will be taken care of properly, and the confidence you will meet their needs.

What do your customers *do* to signal these needs to you?

To help you *identify* when your customers have one or more of these basic needs, indicate below what customers *do or say* that signals one or more needs requires your attention.

What your customers might do or say to signal a basic need	**Message**
_____	
_____	'I need to be understood.'
_____	
_____	
_____	'I need to feel welcome!'
_____	
_____	
_____	'I need to feel important.'
_____	
_____	
_____	'I need to feel comfortable.'
_____	

See the author's comments on what customers commonly do and say to signal these basic needs on page 90.

Step 2
Identify customers' needs by **skilful listening.**

Lisa works in the reservations office of a hotel. She arrives early each morning to take reservations over the telephone. After each call, Lisa always repeats the day of arrival and number of nights of the reservation back to the caller and waits for confirmation. Her listening skills help to keep mistakes at a minimum and customers happy.

Five ways to be a better listener:

1. Stop talking.
2. Avoid distractions.
3. Concentrate on what the other person is saying.
4. Look for the 'real' meaning.
5. Provide feedback to the sender.

'The most important activity any company can do is listen to its customers. Listen hard and listen well – that is the secret to financial success.'

A management consultant

What do you know about listening skills?

Ten faulty assumptions about listening are listed below. Read each carefully and tick those you have previously held.

Don't forget to read carefully the correct assumptions about listening.

Faulty assumptions	**Correct assumptions**
_____ 1. We learn to listen automatically; training is unnecessary.	Effective listening is a skill that is difficult for most of us. Practice and training can improve our ability to listen well.

Faulty assumptions	Correct assumptions
_____ 2. Listening ability depends on intelligence.	There is no relationship between intelligence and listening skill.
_____ 3. Listening ability is closely related to hearing acuity.	Ability to hear is a physcial phenomenon. It has little to do with our ability to listen. In fact, people with hearing loss often make extremely effective listeners.
_____ 4. Generally, most of us can listen well and read something else at the same time.	This is a skill few, if any, people can do effectively.
_____ 5. We listen well most of the time.	Unfortunately, most of us need to work on improving our listening skills.
_____ 6. What we hear is usually what was said.	As human beings, we have a natural tendency to filter information we hear. All too often, what we hear is not what was said.
_____ 7. Listening is a passive action.	Listening is an active process. It requires our _participation_ and _involvement_.
_____ 8. Personality has little effect on listening ability.	Our personality plays an important role in how well we listen.
_____ 9. Listening is done only through the ears.	Effective listening is done with the whole body. Proper eye contact and body posture can facilitate effective listening.
_____ 10. Listening should be concerned with content first and feelings second.	Feelings are often more important than the words themselves. We must look for the underlying feelings in messages. They are often the _real_ message.

Step 2
Identify needs by **obtaining feedback**.

Do you know:

* What your customers want?
* What they need?
* What they think?
* How they feel?
* What suggestions they have?
* Whether they are satisfied?

A family-fun restaurant has initiated an aggressive programme to solicit customer feedback. A dining room employee is assigned the task of personally asking guests at each table to fill in a comment card. If the guests agree, the card is left at the table with a pencil. The guests deposit the card in a box at the front of the restaurant upon leaving. According to the restaurant's manager, several important improvements have been made in the operation as a result of customer suggestions. 'This programme has been invaluable,' she states.

Feedback

Every guest service operation should have ways to obtain feedback from customers. Several methods of finding out what your customers think and feel about the services you provide are listed below. Tick those response methods that are appropriate in your situation, and discuss any questions or ideas you have with your trainer/supervisor.

☐ Listening carefully to what customers/guests or clients have to say.

☐ Checking back regularly to see how things are going.

☐ Making response cards available for customers to comment on service.

☐ Providing a special phone number for guests, customers and/or clients to call for questions, problems or suggestions.

☐ Asking other employees to solicit regular feedback when appropriate.

☐ Ensuring the manager has regular customer contact.

☐ Providing a method that invites customer criticism and responding constructively to any complaints.

☐ Acknowledging all positive comments and reactions as well as any negative ones.

☐ Other: _____

_____

☐ My ideas for improved feedback: _____

_____

Question: What do a telephone company and a car service department have in common?

Answer: They both use phone surveys to find out how satisfied their customers are with the service they received.

Step 2 Summary and follow-up

Summary
The best way to identify the needs of your customers is to try and put yourself in their position, see things from their per-

spective, put yourself in their shoes. This section of the book has outlined a number of suggestions to help you do this.

You can identify the needs of your customers by:

	I do well	Need improvement
• Understanding their human needs	☐	☐
• Knowing their timing requirements	☐	☐
• Anticipating their needs in advance	☐	☐
• Being able to 'read' your customers	☐	☐
• Understanding basic customer needs	☐	☐
• Practising skilful listening	☐	☐
• Obtaining feedback	☐	☐

If at all possible, make a visit to your operation, or one just like it at another location, as a customer. Do everything a customer would do. Make a mental note of what happens at the time and afterwards respond to the following questions:

1. What perspectives did you develop seeing your job from the other side of the fence?
2. How were you treated?
3. What went well?
4. What could have gone better?
5. What insights did you develop that will have a positive impact on how you perform your job?

STEP 3: PROVIDE FOR THE NEEDS OF YOUR CUSTOMERS, GUESTS OR CLIENTS

As an assistant manager in a large retail store, Joe was frustrated with the time and inconvenience of processing customers through the check-out counters. When he finally became manager of his own store, Joe received permission from his district manager to experiment with a new check-out system. The system was so successful, it was adopted throughout the entire chain and Joe received a well-deserved promotion.

What services do you provide?

The first step in providing quality customer service is to recognise and understand all the services that your organisation wants to provide.

Describe below some of the services you will be providing. If you feel your response is incomplete, ask your trainer or supervisor for assistance.

Eight general categories of providing service are listed below. After each, write in specifically what *you will do* to provide service in that particular area. Then add any other services you provide that have not already been listed.

1. Receiving information from customers: _____

_____

_____

_____

2. Providing information to customers: _____

   _____

   _____

   _____

3. Soliciting feedback from customers: _____

   _____

   _____

   _____

4. Following up customers' requests: _____

   _____

   _____

   _____

5. Identifying and solving problems: _____

   _____

   _____

   _____

6. Providing a service for customers: _____

   _____

   _____

   _____

7. Watching or observing: _____

   _____

   _____

   _____

8. Organising: _____

_____

_____

_____

'Each of my major divisions is a service provider for the
other divisions. For example, engineering must design
parts that meet the needs of production. The production
division must gear up to meet the orders from marketing.
And the marketing division must keep engineering
informed of changes in the marketplace. So you see, we
all provide service to each other.'

A corporate CEO

What are the characteristics of the services you provide?

Understanding your *service characteristics* will allow you to
appreciate how the services you provide are seen by your
customers.

Consider these 10 service characteristics:

1. People/Things orientation
Is the service you provide more people oriented or is it more oriented towards things (ie, machines, equipment and technology)?

2. High tech/low tech
If technology is involved in the delivery of the service provided, is it state of the art, or are more traditional tools and/or
systems used?

3. Personal interaction
This characteristic can be divided into three parts:

- *Physical.* Do the parties involved in the service have to see each other? How close are they to each other? What type of touching is involved?
- *Mental.* To what extent does the interaction require the people involved to think, to analyse, to comprehend?
- *Emotional.* To what extent does the interaction rely on emotional-based reactions and/or situations?

4. Time involvement
How long (in duration) does the service take? How *frequently* does it occur?

5. Location
Does the service take place at the customer's site, your location or somewhere else?

6. Complexity

- *Actual.* How complex is the service provided? How complicated are delivery systems?
- *Visual.* How much complexity does the customer see? Do service delivery systems *appear* to be simple when they really are not?

7. Accommodation
How flexible and adaptable are the service systems? To what extent can they be adjusted to meet unique or different customer needs or requests?

8. Numbers served per transaction
How many customers are provided with service during a single service transaction? One or two? A small group? Hundreds? Thousands?

9. Training
How much training, education and/or expertise is needed to deliver service?

10. Supervision
How much supervision does the service system require?

Develop a service profile

Your service profile
Circle the response that most closely matches the nature of the service your service team provides.

1. People/Things orientation	More things	More people
2. Level of technology	High tech	Low tech
3. Personal interaction		
• Physical	High	Low
• Mental	High	Low
• Emotional	High	Low
4. Time involvement		
• Duration	Long	Short
• Frequency	High	Low
5. Location	Their place	Our place
6. Complexity		
• Actual	High	Low
• Visual	High	Low
7. Accommodation ability	High	Low
8. Numbers served per transaction	One	Many

9. Training required	Much	Little
10. Supervision needed	Much	Little

How does this service profile affect the type and level of service you can provide?

_____

_____

Step 3
Provide quality customer service by **performing important back-up duties**.

Back-up duties

Treating customers specially means performing back-up tasks with as much positive energy and interest as you demonstrate in other aspects of your job.

Back-up duties are often shared with colleagues. Lending a hand, doing your fair share, pulling your weight are all part of quality service.

When you are evaluated by your supervisor, you will probably be rated on how well you treat guests, plus on how well you perform the back-up duties.

Common back-up duties include: stocking, filing, recording information, handling telephone calls, assisting with cleaning-up, running errands and/or handling money.

What are some of the back-up tasks you normally perform? List the major ones below:

_____

_____

_____

Check this list with your supervisor to see if you have forgotten anything critical to your job success.

Step 3
Your success will depend on your ability to **send clear messages**.

Ralph runs a neighbourhood bike shop. When taking on new employees for the busy summer season, he tries to tell them as much as he can about bicycles in one day. He does not spend time on training and always promises to write crucial information down, but never seems to find the time. Ralph can't understand why new employees take so long to learn the bicycle business. He laments, 'Good help is hard to find these days.'

The way in which you *communicate* can *make* or *break* your success on the job!

Do you know how to send a message effectively?

If you do, see if you can identify the true statements below:

_____ 1. You should try to impress all customers about how knowledgeable you are.

_____ 2. You should always strive to ensure the self-esteem of your guest.

_____ 3. Repeating the message back to the customer can help to eliminate misunderstandings.

_____ 4. Good eye contact with a guest is rarely important.

_____ 5. When sending a message, it is important to use words that are easily understood.

_____ 6. Silence on the part of a client or guest usually indicates understanding and acceptance of your message.

_____ 7. The more you talk, the better you are at communicating.

_____ 8. Effective communication skills are inborn.

_____ 9. Following up a verbal message with a written message can often facilitate effective communication.

_____10. When coaching or helping a customer or fellow employee, you should focus on behaviour, not on personality.

_____11. Your tone of voice communicates as much, or more, of the message as the words themselves.

_____12. Your body language sends direct messages to others regardless of what you are saying.

_____13. Misunderstanding a customer request is really not a serious problem.

_____14. Effective communication with guests or clients is more important than effective communication among fellow employees.

_____15. Good employees keep their supervisors well-informed at all times.

Answers: True statements are 2, 3, 5, 9, 10, 11, 12, and 15.

'Keep your message short, sweet and to the point. Be specific. Choose the small word over a big one. Work on how to express, not how to impress.'

A communications expert

Step 3
Provide for customer and guest needs by **saying the right thing**.

> A 20-stone man had just finished his dinner at a local steak house when the waiter walked up and said, 'You certainly made that steak disappear fast!' Later, the waiter couldn't understand why the customer complained to the manager.

Saying the right thing

In Step 1 of quality customer service, you used your physical appearance, body language and tone of voice to send a positive attitude.

Now, we must consider the *actual words* to use in order to treat customers as guests.

Even though you have already communicated a great deal by your appearance and body language, it is important to complete your most effective communication skills by selecting the right words to say, and saying them in the right tone of voice.

In the space below write a 'typical' script when you interact with customers while on the job. Include a greeting, the words you would say to handle your transaction, and the way you would conclude the session.

My greeting would be: _____

_____

I would handle the transaction by saying: _____

_____

_____

_____

_____

_____

Once the business had been taken care of, I would say: _____

_____

_____

Review your choice of words with your supervisor or trainer.

Step 3
Satisfying the four basic needs of your customers by

- Showing understanding
- Making them feel welcome
- Helping them to feel important
- Providing a comfortable environment.

The four basic needs of customers

1. The need to be understood
2. The need to feel welcome
3. The need to feel important
4. The need for comfort.

Your success on the job will depend on how well you and your organisation *provide* for these four basic needs, discussed on page 49.

What can you do to provide for these needs?

Fill in your thoughts and ideas on how to provide each of the four basic needs.

1. I plan to show *understanding* by _____

_____

_____

2. I plan to make my guests or customer *feel welcome* by _____

_____

_____

3. I plan to help my customer *feel important* by _____

_____

_____

4. I plan to provide a *comfortable environment* by _____

_____

_____

See the author's comments on page 91.

Step 3
Practise extending your service by effectively selling your organisation's unique products and/or service.

> Beth employs three agents at her travel agency. One agent, Mary Jeanne, books more flights, cruises and tours than the others combined. When asked the secret of her success, Mary Jeanne commented, 'All I do is make my clients aware of the alternatives available to them. I try to be enthusiastic about each option, explaining what I think is important to that client. I also look for the bargains. I want clients to feel they are getting exactly what they want for the lowest price possible. I always try to make them feel good about the plan they choose. They've got to like what they buy or they simply won't come back.'

Selling your customer and/or guests on the quality service you provide is an integral part of your job.
    You sell your service by:

1. Expanding *awareness* of your available services
2. Explaining the *features* of these services
3. Describing the *benefits* of these services.

Please list in the left-hand column below the major services you and your supervisor/trainer listed on page 56.

For each service you list in column 1, write a *feature* or characteristic of that service in column 2, and how that service *benefits* your customer and/or guests in column 3.

1 Services available	2 Features of service	3 Benefits of service

*The next time you mention these services remember to explain the *features* and *benefits*. Your supervisor will be favourably impressed.

Step 3

As time passes, more and more employees will need to learn how to meet the computer challenge.

Computer/Customer relations exercise

An increasing number of jobs require you to meet the service needs of your customers through the use of a computer.

The computer (which is an object) requires your attention and skill, *but not at the expense of guests and/or customers*.

Five statements about computers and customer/client relations are presented below. Read each and indicate your agreement or disagreement. Then briefly explain the reasoning for your response.

Statement		Reasoning
1. Operating a terminal may at first be so difficult that your ability to provide quality service is adversely affected.	Agree Disagree Because:	_____ _____ _____
2. Operating the computer properly is often more important than treating a customer as a guest.	Agree Disagree Because:	_____ _____ _____
3. When you have problems with the computer, the best thing to do is to concentrate absolutely in order to work out the problem.	Agree Disagree Because:	_____ _____ _____
4. Operating a computer terminal requires you to split concentration between it and a customer/guest.	Agree Disagree Because:	_____ _____ _____

5. If your transaction is long and
   involved, you should always let
   your customer know, and then com-   Agree   _____
   pensate by being empathetic and   Disagree _____
   friendly.   Because: _____

Compare your comments with those of the author on page 92.

Prepare for the unexpected

Everything doesn't always go as planned: a shipment is
delayed, a key employee is ill, a newspaper ad carries an incor-
rect price. When the unexpected happens (and it will), the
organisation that is most concerned with customer service will
usually come out ahead. The best approach is to think ahead to
what might go wrong – and consider some back-up scenarios.

A California corporation has just initiated an earthquake
preparedness programme. Contingency plans have been
fully developed for keeping services flowing in case the
'big one' hits.

Step 3
Providing quality customer service may be especially challenging
when the unexpected happens.

Unexpected occurrences often place extra burdens on your
ability to deliver quality customer service. They may present a
formidable challenge.

While all possible occurrences may not be foreseen, common or expected situations can be anticipated. In these cases,
contingency plans can be developed to help you do your job
under these possible abnormal circumstances.

A number of possible unexpected occurrences are listed
below. Circle the ones that *could possibly apply in your situation*

and indicate any contingency action plans that could be followed to help maintain quality customer service. Discuss your ideas with your supervisor.

The unexpected	Your contingency plan
1. Foul weather	_____
2. Loss of power	_____
3. Equipment failure	_____
4. Computer breakdown	_____
5. Overcrowded conditions	_____
6. Understaffing	_____
7. Fire/Health emergency	_____
8. Air conditioning/central heating control malfunction	_____
9. Phones down	_____
10. Needed supplies exhausted	_____
11. Breakdown in the delivery system	_____
12. Other; you add:	
_____	_____

Step 3 Summary and follow-up
You can provide for the needs of your customers by:

- Performing *all* the tasks and duties required of your job
- Performing important back-up duties
- Communicating by sending clear messages, to:
  —Customers
  —Supervisors; and
  —Fellow employees

- Making only appropriate comments to customers
- Satisfying the four basic needs of your customers
- Practising effective selling skills
- Meeting the computer challenge
- Continuing to deliver quality customer service when the unexpected occurs.

STEP 4: MAKE SURE YOUR CUSTOMERS, CLIENTS AND/OR GUESTS RETURN

Whether a customer purchases a complete wardrobe or only a tie, one medium-size department store makes it a policy to follow up each sale with a brief thank-you note. The chairman of the company says. 'Such a policy encourages customers to return, and that's what makes our business thrive.'

What you can do to make sure customers come back

On the facing page is a list of items you can do personally to make sure that customers return.

Some interesting statistics tell why companies lose customers:*

1% of lost customers die.
3% move away.
4% just naturally float.
5% change on a friend's recommendations.
9% can buy it cheaper somewhere else.
10% are chronic complainers.
68% go elsewhere because the people they deal with are indifferent to their needs.

Customers are not the icing on the cake – they *are* the cake. The icing is an improved reputation and higher profits as a result of a quality job.

---

*Reprinted from *Quality at Work* (Kogan Page).

Making sure customers return

Rank those items that apply to your job in order of importance and then ask your supervisor to do the same. Compare the responses and discuss any differences.

Your rankings		**Your supervisor's rankings**
_____	1. Always be pleasant to customers even if they are not pleasant to you.	_____
_____	2. Welcome customer/guest suggestions about how you could improve in your job.	_____
_____	3. Graciously receive and handle any complaints or problems.	_____
_____	4. Go 'above and beyond' to care for a customer.	_____
_____	5. Smile even during those times when you don't feel like it.	_____
_____	6. Roll with the punches, accepting bad news or tight schedules calmly.	_____
_____	7. Provide service that is beyond what customers expect from you.	_____
_____	8. Provide helpful suggestions and/or guidance when you feel customers need it.	_____
_____	9. Thoroughly explain the features and benefits for all of the services you provide.	_____
_____	10. Follow through to ensure that your customer commitments are honoured.	_____

> Statistics say it costs six times more to attract a new cus-
> tomer than to keep a current one.

Step 4
Make sure customers return by doing what you can to **satisfy those who complain**.

Handling complaints

Steps you should take
1. *Listen* carefully to the complaint.
2. *Repeat* the complaint back and get acknowledgement that you heard it correctly.
3. *Apologise.*
4. *Acknowledge* the customer's or guest's feelings (anger, frustration, disappointment, etc).
5. *Explain* what action you will take to correct the problem.
6. *Thank* the customer for bringing the problem to your attention.

Situation – front desk
A guest approaches the front desk of your hotel and is visibly upset. He informs you that the room you just assigned to him is 'uninhabitable' because it smells strongly of cigarette smoke. Neither he nor his wife smokes and the odour is nauseating. He informs you that he feels a hotel of this calibre and price should have no-smoking rooms. He demands immediate action.

What would you say to this guest?

Record your action plan below:

Action
Repeat the complaint: _____

_____

Apologise: _____

Acknowledge the feelings: _____

_____

Explain what you will do: _____

_____

Thank the guest: _____

_____

See the author's comments on page 92.

Common complaints

Most customer service operations often find that customers tend to complain about some things more than others.

Do you know what these most common complaints are?

Do you know what to *do* and what to *say* when you are faced with one?

Discuss complaints with your supervisor before you fill this in.

Use the left-hand column below to list the most common customer complaints you can anticipate facing on your job.

For each complaint you list on the left, indicate, on the right, how you should handle the complaint. This includes (1) what you would do and (2) what you would say.

Common complaints	Recommended action
_____	_____
_____	_____
_____	_____
_____	_____
_____	_____

Types of difficult customers with whom you may have to deal

- The angry customer
- The nasty or obnoxious person
- The seething but silent individual
- The demanding client
- The constant critic
- The non-stop talker
- The weirdo.
- The indecisive person
- The intoxicated guest
- The argumentative patient.

Your addition: _____

_____

Why are these people difficult?

Most difficult people are operating from a base of *insecurity*. Like all of us, they, too, have a need to be understood, feel welcome, comfortable and important.

Difficult people are often merely expressing a need, although they are choosing an inappropriate and impolite way to communicate this need.

They are being difficult for their own reasons – not because of you.

Here are some common reasons why customers may be difficult. Tick the ones that may apply to you and your situation.

_____ 1. They are tired or frustrated.

_____ 2. They are confused or overwhelmed.

_____ 3. They are defending their ego or self-esteem.

_____ 4. They have never been in a similar situation before.

_____ 5. They feel ignored. Nobody has listened to them.

_____ 6. They may be under the influence of alcohol or drugs.

_____ 7. They don't speak or understand the language very well.

_____ 8. They have been treated poorly in similar circumstances in the past.

_____ 9. They are in a bad mood and take it out on you.

_____ 10. They are in a hurry or have waited a long time for service.

_____ 11. Other; you specify _____

_____

Step 4
Make sure customers return by learning to **get difficult customers on your side**.

1. Don't take it personally
This is one of the hardest customer-service skills to learn. Remember, they are not attacking you personally (even though it may seem that they are).

2. Remain calm; listen carefully
This is easy to say here, but difficult to do. Take a deep breath and plan your words carefully. Paraphrase what they have said to make sure you have heard them correctly.

3. Focus on the problem, not the person
Go to a quiet area. Sit down. Be a problem solver. Try to work out what this person needs and satisfy this need in some way, if you can. Let them know what you *can do*.

4. Reward yourself for turning a difficult customer into a happy one

Case 2
The difficult customer

Situation – airline ticket counter

A middle-aged woman approaches the ticket counter of an airline at a large airport and demands to see the manager. You ask if you can be of any assistance since the manager is not available.

She immediately challenges the airline's no-pet policy as unfair and discriminatory. She explains that she has to travel 1000 miles to attend a sick sister. Her toy poodle, from whom she has never been separated, is completely house trained and 'never barks or bites.' She can't stand the thought of her 'little baby' all alone in the dangerous, cold and dark baggage compartment. After all, 'dogs can freeze up there and there may not be enough air to breathe'. She is holding the dog tightly in her arms. The pooch is clothed in a designer jacket made for small dogs and has her nails polished bright red. The lady loudly demands she be allowed to bring her pet on board with her.

What should you do? Place a cross in the box of the actions below that are the most appropriate response to this difficult situation:

☐ 1. Show slight disgust on your face so she will know you consider *her* to be the problem.

☐ 2. Laugh and make light of the situation.

☐ 3. Remain calm, cool and patient.

☐ 4. Sympathise with her feelings of fear and frustration. Tell her that you don't like to leave your pets alone either.

☐ 5. Walk away to find the manager.

☐ 6. Become distant and less cooperative.

☐ 7. Disarm her by asking, 'Are you serious?'

☐ 8. Explain carefully about the gentle treatment pets receive in the pet compartment and how many pets fly with your airline each day.

☐ 9. Ask her to understand the airline's need to consider all the passengers.

☐ 10. Thank her for understanding and cooperating.

See the author's comments on page 92.

When you find yourself confronted with a difficult situation that you don't know how to handle, involve your supervisor.

Certain problems may require your supervisor to handle them. If so, find out what these problem areas are, and observe how they are handled.

Step 4
Make sure customers will return by taking that **one extra service step.**

Patty, a part-time employee in a local gift shop, was helping a young woman in a hurry. While the woman was looking for the right card, Patty was wrapping the gift to which the card would be attached. Suddenly, Patty realised that the customer was taking the gift directly with her and said, 'You will need a pen to sign the card. Here, take this one with you.' The customer said in surprise, 'Yes. How did you know? Thank you very much.'

Surprise your customers!

Treat them as guests! Go beyond what they expect!

Examples

Ticket agent:	'Would you like me to select a seat for your return flight now?'
Salesperson:	'I'll deliver it personally this afternoon.'
Night nurse:	'Since you are awake, let me find some lemonade for you to drink.'
Bank loan officer:	'I don't know the answer now, but I'll call you back before 11 am with the answer.'
Waitress:	'May I bring extra glasses so you can try both wines?'
Hotel desk clerk:	'May I call a cab for you?'
Car mechanic:	'Since your car will take longer than planned, may I give you a lift home?'
Receptionist in a government agency:	'To avoid your getting lost on the third floor, let me draw a map for you.'
Grocer's assistant:	'Let me get you some help to carry out your groceries.'
Bank clerk:	'Take this new cheque-book cover. Yours looks a little worn.'

How can *you* take that extra step of service?

List ways you feel would be appropriate for your job. Then show the list to your supervisor for his/her reaction.

1. _____
2. _____
3. _____
4. _____
5. _____
6. _____
7. _____
8. _____
9. _____
10. _____

Step 4. Summary and follow-up
Make sure your customers, clients and/or guests return by:

- Working to satisfy customer complaints
- Being prepared to handle the most common complaints properly.
- Learning to get difficult customers on your side
- Understanding why some customers are more difficult than others
- Taking that one extra step to provide quality customer service
- Consistently practising *all* the principles of quality customer service that you have learned about in this book.

CHAPTER 3
Check Your Progress

True or False

_____ 1. People who are successful at customer relations constantly need to be the centre of attention.

_____ 2. Treating customers as guests means viewing your job primarily as a human relations representative.

_____ 3. Guest service employees are at the mercy of their customers, and thus have little control over their success on the job.

_____ 4. Treating customers as guests often means apologising for mistakes you did not make.

_____ 5. It isn't really important to remember the names and faces of your customers.

_____ 6. If you have limited desire to please others, you probably shouldn't be in a service-related job.

_____ 7. How you handle the procedural (or technical) side of your job can directly affect how you handle the personal side.

_____ 8. Knowing the time requirements for providing quality service will help you to do a better job.

_____ 9. Good anticipation means providing items and services for customers without requiring them to ask.

_____ 10. When communicating with another person, is is always important to consider and protect his or her self-esteem.

_____ 11. Eye contact has little impact on good communication.

_____ 12. Feedback rarely provides the information necessary to do a better job.

_____ 13. If you are not careful, working on a computer can adversely affect your attentiveness towards customers/guests.

_____ 14. Generally, the attitude you receive from others is the same attitude you transmit.

_____ 15. Reading the customer correctly can pay great dividends for you and your organisation.

_____ 16. Most people simply want fast service and have little need to feel important or be recognised.

_____ 17. Body language often communicates more than the actual words you use.

_____ 18. When a guest is rude, obnoxious and impolite, it is justifiable for you to return the same behaviour.

_____ 19. It is really impractical to think that you should try to go one step beyond the expectations of those you serve.

_____ 20. Customer complaints should be encouraged.

Answers on page 93.

Follow-up

You have now completed this programme. This is an excellent time to sit down with your manager and/or trainer and talk about what you have learned. This is also a good time to clarify any questions you may have about the job.

Tell your manager you have completed the programme and ask for time to discuss it.

Use the space opposite to make notes about what you want to talk about or questions you still have.

Things to discuss

1.

2.

3.

4.

5.

6.

CHAPTER 4
Author's Notes and Comments

Body language exercise (page 32)

Positive messages

Face is relaxed and under control. This communicates that you are prepared, know what you are doing, and/or are comfortable with your role.

Smile is natural and comfortable. This communicates that you are sure of yourself, like what you are doing and enjoy your guests.

Eye contact is maintained when talking and listening to guests. This communicates that guests are important, you are interested in them and are self-confident.

Body movement is relaxed, yet deliberate and controlled. This communicates that you are in control, you are glad to be where you are and that, although you are busy, that's just part of the job.

Negative messages

Face is anxious and uptight. This communicates that you are ill prepared, inexperienced and/or uncomfortable with your role.

Smile is missing or forced. This communicates that you are unsure of yourself, don't like what you are doing, and/or really don't enjoy your guests.

Eye contact is avoided when talking and listening to customers. This communicates a lack of interest in the guest, and/or you lack the self-confidence to do the job.

Body movement is harried and rushed. This communicates that you are not in control of the situation, and would really like the guests to leave.

Listening to the sound of your own voice (page 34)

The tone of voice that is conducive to your success in customer relations can be described by any of these four characteristics:

1. It is upbeat.
2. It is warm, comfortable and understanding.
3. It is under control.
4. It is clear, direct and natural.

Case 1. Thelma's performance appraisal (page 40)

Is Thelma a good employee?
The answer is both 'yes' and 'no'. She certainly does half of her job well – the non-people side. When it comes to interacting with customers, a very important part of the job, Thelma is not a good employee.

Is the manager justified in his recommendations?
Answer: I think so. He cannot afford someone like Thelma turning off customers. His business relies on warm, friendly customer relations.

What suggestions would you make to Thelma?
Answer: Learn and practise the principles of quality customer service as soon as possible or seek a position behind the scenes or elsewhere that won't require customer interaction.

Timeliness (page 44)

The value of this exercise is to establish clear timeliness expectations between you and your supervisor or trainer. You may have your own ideas of what is timely, but it is more important to find out what your supervisor considers to be timely. In fact, your job may depend upon it.

Anticipate customer needs (page 46)

Situation	Anticipated need
A customer has waited longer than normal for service.	An extra warm smile. A verbal recognition of the extended wait. A comment of appreciation for waiting. Speedy service.
A client keeps looking at his watch.	This person may have a train to catch or another appointment. Recognise this need and provide prompt service.
A woman guest with three small children.	Provide some items to occupy the children while they wait.
Queues for service form early.	Have appropriate supplies and equipment on hand. Have enough staff to meet the demand.
You have well-defined busy periods.	Prepare yourself mentally and physically. Don't be caught off guard.

Reading the customer exercise (page 48)

Age of customer

Young:	Some young customers may be inexperienced or unsure of themselves. Explain things clearly. Be patient and set them at ease.
Old:	Seniors appreciate a friendly comment or two. Make casual conversation. Show some interest and attention.

Type of clothing

High fashion: Show well-dressed people the respect and deference they expect.

Out-of-fashion: Help these people to feel welcome and comfortable.

Verbal ability

Extremely fluent: Listen carefully. Paraphrase back what you hear.

Barely fluent: Listen carefully. Explain things simply and clearly.

Attitude

Positive: Recognise and encourage it.

Negative: Be positive and understanding. Show empathy.

Impatient

Be as prompt as you can. Explain what's happening. Explain how long the process will take. Be polite.

Demanding or angry

Be polite and patient. Listen carefully. Stay calm. Show understanding.

Four basic needs (page 49)

Customers express these four needs in a variety of ways. Here are just a few of them.

1. The need to be understood

This need is signalled by customers repeating themselves; speaking slowly; speaking loudly; getting angry when they are not being understood, or bringing a friend or relative to help explain.

2. The need to feel welcome
This need is signalled by 'looking around' before coming in and/or coming in with friends or relatives. It is also demonstrated by wearing the 'right' clothes for the situation.

3. The need to feel important
This need is often signalled by someone showing off or bragging about who they know. This need is also demonstrated by flashing money about, a display of jewellery and/or extreme clothing.

4. The need for comfort
This need is expressed by customers being ill at ease, nervous, or unsure of themselves when feeling uncomfortable. This need is also expressed when help, assistance or directions are requested.

Satisfying basic customer needs (page 65)

1. The need to be understood
Paraphrase back what is being said. Listen for feelings communicated as well as the content of the message. Empathise with problems or predicaments.

2. The need to feel welcome
Provide a warm and friendly welcome. Use a vocabulary everyone will understand. Engage in friendly conversation.

3. The need to feel important
Learn to address others by name. Do something special. Tune in to individual needs.

4. The need for comfort
Set customers at ease. Relieve anxiety. Explain the service procedures carefully and calmly.

Computer/Customer relations exercise (page 68)

1. *Agree.* You may sacrifice valuable customer time getting the computer to work properly. If you can practise on the computer before hours or during slow periods, this problem should be minimised.
2. *Disagree.* You must learn to treat customers as guests *and* operate the computer properly. Both are vital to your job success.
3. *Disagree.* Never concentrate on a computer problem *at the expense of a customer*. Get some assistance right away.
4. *Agree.* This is true; however, operating the computer soon becomes second nature. When this happens, you will be able to focus most of your attention on the customers.
5. *Agree.* Always let your client know what is going on. Sometimes a wait or delay doesn't seem quite as long when you have received an explanation for the delay.

Handling complaints (page 74)

A possible dialogue might go something like this:
'Your room smells strongly of cigarette smoke.' (Repeating the complaint.) 'I'm very sorry, sir.' (Apology.) 'You certainly have a right to be upset. I would be too.' (Acknowledgement of feelings.) 'What I would like to do, if it is all right with you, is move you and your wife to another room right away. I'll have a porter assist you.' (Explaining the action that you will take.) 'Would that be all right?'
Guest: 'Much better.'
'Thank you for bringing this to my attention. I'm glad you told me about it. It should not have happened.' (Thanking the guest.)

The difficult customer (page 78)

The correct responses to this situation would be to:

3. Remain calm, cool and patient.
4. Recognise the feelings of frustration and fear she expressed by telling her that you don't like to leave your pets alone either.
8. Tell her about the gentle treatment pets receive in the pet compartment and how many pets fly with your airline each day.
10. Thank her for understanding and cooperating.

Review True-False test (page 83)

1. F (Treating customers as guests means to make *them* the centre of attention.) 2. T 3. F (You have almost complete control over your job success.) 4. T 5. F (Remembering names and faces is one of the most important things you can do.) 6. T 7. T 8. T 9. T 10. T 11. F (Eye contact has a great impact on communication.) 12. F (Client feedback provides invaluable information.) 13. T 14. T 15. T 16. F (Most people want to be served quickly and efficiently *and* need to feel important and recognised.) 17. T 18. F (It is never justifiable to be rude or short with a guest.) 19. F (Going one step beyond the expectations of your guests should become a natural extension of your job.) 20. T

To the supervisor and/or trainer

Quality Customer Service has been designed to make your job as a trainer more effective, and, hopefully a bit easier. This book is *not* intended to replace on-the-job training. Its purpose is to set the stage for more efficient hands-on training.

Flexibility

This book breaks the art of treating customers as guests into four simple steps: (1) transmitting a positive attitude; (2) identifying customer needs; (3) providing for customer needs; and (4) cultivating repeat business. Ideally, the trainee will complete each step *before* actual customer contact, although these learning steps can be used effectively at any time.

If you are using *Quality Customer Service* to complement other training that is taking place, each step may be assigned independently or in concert with other sessions. The programme is highly adaptable and can be used with most training programmes.

Feedback and discussion

Trainee will want to discuss the exercises in the book. Questions will arise that only you can answer. The following sections in the book suggest your involvement.

1. A discussion of the case, 'Thelma's Performance Appraisal', (page 40) is helpful and will serve as a general review of Step 1.
2. The 'Timeliness' exercise on page 44 asks for your input based on the specific timing requirements of your organisation.
3. The trainee may need help in listing all the services he/she will be providing as well as services provided by others on page 56. You may also want to review the trainee's script for handling a customer transaction on page 61.

4. Following pages 74 and 78, you may wish to discuss the policies and procedures you have for handling customer complaints or difficult guests.

Upon completion of the programme

A follow-up session between you and the trainee is suggested at the end of the programme. To make the session most effective, you should arrange a meeting and discuss each section of the book. The feedback that follows should help you to establish a supportive relationship with your employee. The time you devote to these sessions will be well invested.

Further reading from Kogan Page

Customer Care, Sarah Cook, 1992
Customer Service, Malcolm Peel, revised 1993
Inspired Customer Service, Colin Armistead, David Clutterbuck
  and Graham Clark, 1993
Keeping Customers for Life, Richard F Gerson, 1993
Managing Quality Customer Service, William B Morris, 1991
Measuring Customer Satisfaction, Richard F Gerson, 1994